HIGHLY ESTEEMED
A STUDY OF DANIEL

BIBLE STUDIES TO IMPACT THE LIVES OF ORDINARY PEOPLE

Written by Dorothy Russell

The Word Worldwide

CHRISTIAN FOCUS

For details of our titles visit us on our website
www.christianfocus.com

ISBN 1-84550-006-7

Copyright © WEC International
Published in 2004 by
Christian Focus Publications Ltd, Geanies House,
Fearn, Tain, Ross-shire, IV20 ITW, Scotland
and
WEC International, Bulstrode, Oxford Road,
Gerrards Cross, Bucks, SL9 8SZ

Cover design by Alister MacInnes

Printed and bound by Bell & Bain, Glasgow

CONTENTS

PREFACE 4
INTRODUCTORY STUDY 5

QUESTIONS AND NOTES

STUDY 1 – GOD NEVER FAILS 7
STUDY 2 – MAN IS HELPLESS – GOD IS ALL-POWERFUL 10
STUDY 3 – OUR GOD IS ABLE 13
STUDY 4 – A MAN WHO FOUND GOD 17
STUDY 5 – THE NATION THAT LOST GOD 21
STUDY 6 – A MAN OF PRAYER 25
STUDY 7 – WHAT IS THE WORLD COMING TO? 28
STUDY 8 – GOD ALLOWS A GLIMPSE INTO THE FUTURE 31
STUDY 9 – ANSWERED PRAYER 35
STUDY 10 – SPIRITUAL WARFARE 39
STUDY 11 – HISTORY LESSON ... IN ADVANCE 42
STUDY 12 – DANIEL WILL BE THERE – WILL YOU? 46

ANSWER GUIDE

STUDY 1 50
STUDY 2 51
STUDY 3 52
STUDY 4 53
STUDY 5 54
STUDY 6 55
STUDY 7 56
STUDY 8 57
STUDY 9 58
STUDY 10 59
STUDY 11 60
STUDY 12 61

PREFACE

GEARED FOR GROWTH

'Where there's LIFE there's GROWTH:
Where there's GROWTH there's LIFE.'

WHY GROW a study group?

Because as we study the Bible and share together we can

- learn to combat loneliness, depression, staleness, frustration, and other problems
- get to understand and love each other
- become responsive to the Holy Spirit's dealing and obedient to God's Word

and that's GROWTH.

How do you GROW a study group?

- Just start by asking a friend to join you and then aim at expanding your group.
- Study the set portions daily (they are brief and easy: no catches).
- Meet once a week to discuss what you find.
- Befriend others, both Christians and non-Christians, and work away together

see how it GROWS!

WHEN you GROW ...

This will happen at school, at home, at work, at play, in your youth group, your student fellowship, women's meetings, mid-week meetings, churches and communities,

you'll be REACHING THROUGH TEACHING

INTRODUCTORY STUDY

Begin this study by sharing, as a group, anything you already know about Daniel.
Have you ever heard it said that 'history' is 'His-story', i.e., God's story? The message of the book of Daniel is just this: God is sovereign and in control of history, from beginning to end.
So we must see this book set in its historical context, in relation to:
A. What has gone before,
B. The history of the time,
C. What comes after.

A. What has gone before
When **DAVID** was king of the nation of Israel, God promised that his house and his kingdom would be established for ever.
The sins of **SOLOMON** (David's son), and his son **REHOBOAM**, caused the kingdom to be torn in two – Israel (the northern part) and Judah (the southern part)
The kingdom of **Israel** sinned against God so much, that Divine judgment came in the form of the Assyrians, and the people were carried captive to ASSYRIA in 721 BC
The kingdom of **Judah** failed to learn from the mistakes of Israel, and also turned away from God. King Nebuchadnezzar was the instrument of God's judgment, and after a series of invasions, the people were finally deported to BABYLON in 586 BC.
Read Daniel chapter 1 verses 1-6 to see where our story begins.

B. The history of the time
From the following references list the kings who ruled in Babylon during Daniel's lifetime?
Daniel 2:1; Daniel 5:1; Daniel 5:30-31; Daniel 6:28

Jeremiah 25:1, 2, 8-11. Where did Jeremiah the prophet live during this time?

Jeremiah 29:1, 4-7. To whom did he write a letter on one occasion?

Ezekiel 1:1-3. Where did the prophet Ezekiel live and prophesy?

Psalm 137:1-6. How did the exiled people of Judah feel?

C. What comes after
Jeremiah 29:10-14. What did God show the prophet Jeremiah about the future of Judah?

Isaiah 44:26–45:4. What did He reveal to Isaiah?

Ezra 1:1-4; Psalm 126:1-3. What, in fact, happened when Cyrus became king?

2 Kings 24 and 25, and 2 Chronicles 36 also record historical events of this period. You may like to read them at home.

Look at the names of the books of the Bible that have already been referred to in this study. How many can you find?

So much is written in God's Word about those seventy years known as 'The Exile', that we can surely see what a significant time it was in God's sovereign purpose.

What kind of a man was Daniel?
How did Ezekiel describe him (Ezek. 14:14, 20; 28:3)?

What important characteristic is brought out in Daniel 6:10; 9:20?

How did the Divine Being in his vision address him in Daniel 10:11?

What did Jesus refer to him as (Matt. 24:15)?

What does the writer to the Hebrews tell us about this man who shut the mouths of lions? (Heb. 11:32, 33).

A Riddle!
Why was Daniel like a nice, ripe fig (Jer. 24:1-5)?

STUDY 1
GOD NEVER FAILS

QUESTIONS

DAY 1 *Daniel 1:1-3.*
a) Why was Nebuchadnezzar successful against Jehoiakim and what did he do?

b) Nebuchadnezzar invaded Judah and Jerusalem several more times (2 Chron. 36:5-11, 17-23). What happened on each occasion?

DAY 2 *Daniel 1:3-7.*
a) What do we know about Daniel's parents?

b) Why were Daniel and his three friends chosen to enter the king's service?

DAY 3 *Daniel 1:4-7.*
a) What course of study were the young men to follow?

b) The endings '-el' and '-iah' in Hebrew were names for God. 'Bel' (Baal), 'Achu' and 'Negu' were names of the gods worshipped in Babylon. What do you think the king was trying to do by changing their names?

DAY 4 *Daniel 1:8-10.*
a) Here was Daniel's first test of faith. What motivated him to seek a change in diet?

QUESTIONS (contd.)

b) How does I Corinthians 10:18-21 help us understand Daniel's objection to the king's food and wine?

DAY 5 *Daniel 1:8-14.*
a) What steps did Daniel take to avoid defilement?

b) What example does Daniel set on how to deal with situations we want to see changed?

DAY 6 *Daniel 1:8-16.*
a) Which part of I Samuel 2:30 had come true for Daniel? How might this encourage us?

b) Think of a country where Christians are being persecuted and pray that people in key government positions will become sympathetic to them.

c) Why were Daniel and his three friends allowed to continue with their vegetable diet?

DAY 7 *Daniel 1:15-21.*
a) How again did God work in Daniel's situation?

b) What effect would this have had on all the other Israelite captives?

NOTES

HOME INFLUENCE (where decisions are made for us)
The influence of a godly home on young children and young people cannot be over estimated. The whole story of Daniel hinges on the fact that his parents trained him up 'in the way he should go' (Prov. 22:6).

Is this a challenge to you? If you have children at home you have a responsibility to teach them about the Lord Jesus. Talk about your own faith, and pray with them. Don't leave it all to the Sunday School! Ask the Lord if you are doing everything possible to give them a sound Christian foundation for their lives.

TEENAGE YEARS (when we begin to make decisions for ourselves)
Daniel was probably in his late teens when he (through no choice of his own) left home, and found himself enrolled in a three year Science and Literature Course at the University of Babylon. He was ready to accept this education, and even a change of name, but when it came to doing something which God, in His Word, had expressly forbidden, he stood against it and made the right decision.

If you have teenagers who have gone to University or are living away from home for any reason, you have a vitally important responsibility. It is to pray for them every day, that they will be willing to go God's way, and make right decisions.

If you are a young person, remember that the very first decision Daniel made was to influence his whole future life. Make your stand for the Lord and people will know just where you stand. David Pawson says, 'Because he wouldn't eat the king's meat when he was nineteen, the lions wouldn't eat him when he was ninety!'

ADULT LIFE (when God holds us responsible for the decisions we make)
God has made a promise: 'Those who honour me, I will honour' (I Sam. 2:30).

God honoured Daniel and his friends by giving them physical health, superior knowledge and understanding, because these things would equip them for the work God had for them to do in that heathen kingdom.

If you take a stand for God, and honour Him, either on a personal or social moral issue, God will honour you in the way best suited to your situation. At every stage in our lives, if we faithfully do the will of God and put our trust in Him, we will find that **God never fails.**

STUDY 2
MAN IS HELPLESS – GOD IS ALL-POWERFUL

QUESTIONS

DAY 1 *Daniel 2:1-11.*
a) What initially troubled Nebuchadnezzar's mind? What irritated him still further?

b) In what terms did the astrologers finally admit their helplessness (v. 11)?

DAY 2 *Daniel 2:12-18.*
a) What dangerous situation did Daniel find himself in?

b) How did Daniel react to this?

c) What lessons can we learn from Daniel's action in verses 17-18?

DAY 3 *Daniel 2:19-23; 1:17.*
a) How did God answer the prayer of Daniel and his friends?

b) How did Daniel react to this? Put in your own words what he said about God.

DAY 4 *Daniel 2:24-30; Genesis 41:15-16.*
a) How did Daniel describe God to Nebuchadnezzar? What was he careful to say about himself?

QUESTIONS (contd.)

b) How did Daniel briefly summarise the dream for Nebuchadnezzar?

DAY 5 *Read Daniel 2:31-35, then close your Bible and seek to answer:*
a) What was the head made of? The chest and arms? The waist and hips?

b) What were the legs made of? The feet?

c) What do you notice about the order in which these metals are placed?

DAY 6 *Daniel 2:36-45.*
a) How is the rock, or stone, described by Daniel? What impact does it have on the other kingdoms?

b) How does Psalm 118:22-23, Matthew 21:42-46 and Acts 4:10-11 increase our understanding of the meaning of the rock, or stone?

DAY 7 *Daniel 2:46-49.*
a) What three things did King Nebuchadnezzar learn about God from his dream as a result of Daniel having explained it?

b) What honours were bestowed on Daniel?

c) What did he request?

How **helpless** those magicians, enchanters, sorcerers and astrologers were, faced with a situation they couldn't bluff their way through!

How **helpless** King Nebuchadnezzar was, in spite of his position as ruler over a flourishing empire!

How **helpless** Daniel would have been ... without God.

How **helpless** that enormous statue, symbolising the great Ages of Man, eventually was, crushed to powder by The Stone.

Nebuchadnezzar seemed to be **all-powerful** (gold). He had 'dominion and power and might and glory' (v. 37). Babylon was celebrated for its wealth and grandeur, and was the symbol of luxury and pride. It had continued as a kingdom since Sargon I, almost 2,000 years before.

The kingdom of the Medes and Persians conquered Babylon in 536 BC. To have overcome the greatest empire on earth, suggested great power. But though the Persian kingdom was greater in size, it could not match the grandeur of Babylon, and its form of government was very much inferior (silver). Morality, also, declined.

Greece overthrew the Medo-Persian empire in 330 BC, and the power of Alexander the Great extended 'over the whole earth' . He is reported to have wept because there were no more worlds left to conquer! His rule was by the sword; he acquired his authority by military skill (bronze) but he died at the age of thirty-two as a result of his drunken and licentious lifestyle.

Rome's **power** ruled the world from 65 BC. It is represented in the dream as the legs of iron – very appropriate, as the Romans constructed solid roads and their soldiers marched to every corner of the empire.

BUT ... the Stone is **all-powerful.**

Christ will come, breaking into history, bringing devastating judgment on all that stands in His way. Unbelieving nations will continue to reject the grace of God in Jesus Christ until the day when He comes in power and great glory (Matt. 24:30). Then, as Isaiah prophesied: 'They will neither harm nor destroy on all my holy mountain,' says the Lord, 'for the earth will be full of the knowledge of the LORD as the waters cover the sea' (Isa. 11:9).

The final scene in this drama shows this supposedly all-powerful king bowing down before his Hebrew servant, and then giving him a position of power and authority. We can catch a glimpse of the One who took 'the very nature of a servant, being made in human likeness. And being found in appearance as a man he humbled himself ....

Therefore God exalted him to the highest place and gave him the name that is above every name, that at the name of Jesus every knee should bow' (Phil. 2:7-10).

STUDY 3
OUR GOD IS ABLE

QUESTIONS

DAY 1 *Daniel 3:1-7.*
a) Why did Nebuchadnezzar summon all his officials to Babylon?

b) Why would it be difficult to resist the order to worship the image?

DAY 2 *Daniel 3:8-12.*
a) Who were identified as having flouted the king's order?

b) Why do you think these men were eager to bring this accusation?

DAY 3 *Daniel 3:13-18.*
a) What opinion had Nebuchadnezzar of himself (v. 15b)?

b) How did Shadrach, Meshach and Adednego respond to the king's threat?

c) Luke 12:11-12. What encouragement do Christians have when they are being persecuted?

DAY 4 *Daniel 3:16-18*
a) Pick out the phrases that show:
their FAITH in God's power,

their ASSURANCE of His care,

QUESTIONS (contd.)

their ACCEPTANCE of His will,

their OBEDIENCE to Him.

b) What example have these three men set for us?

DAY 5 *Daniel 3:19-25; Isaiah 43:2-3.*
a) How did the king show how furious he was?

b) What three things later amazed the king?

DAY 6 *Daniel 3:26-28; Hebrews 11:32-38.*
a) Who witnessed this amazing demonstration of the power of God?

b) Discuss why you think God worked this miracle, considering the many martyrs burned at the stake in later years.

DAY 7 *Daniel 3:28-30; Revelation 12:11.*
a) What did the king say about God?

b) What did the king say about Shadrach, Meshach and Abednego?

c) What part of this week's study has impressed you most?

NOTES

Interviewer This programme comes to you from our studio. We are fortunate to have with us Shadrach, Meshach and Abednego who have survived what must be one of the most horrific experiences one could have. We have heard the report of their ordeal on the news, and now I would like to ask them a few questions : Tell us how you felt when you first heard the king's command.

Shadrach We immediately thought of God's command not to make an idol, or image, or bow down to it or worship it. We knew from the start that we had to obey God rather than men.

Interviewer As you saw the great preparations being made, the building of the enormous statue covered in gold, the musicians practising on their instruments, and the people arriving from every corner of the province – were you not even a little scared?

Meshach Many of our forefathers – Abraham, Joseph and David, to mention a few – had their faith tested to the limits, and won through. This was to be our test. Could we not trust the God of our fathers?

Interviewer But what about that blazing furnace? Surely that must have made you tremble in fear.

Abednego We thought at once of what God had said through one of our contemporary prophets, Isaiah: 'Fear not ... you are mine. When you pass through the waters, I will be with you.... When you walk through the fire, you will not be burned; the flames will not set you ablaze.' And as you know, the Holy One was right there in the fire with us.

Interviewer Well, I must say I admire your courage. But tell me, when you were brought before the king, did he give you an opportunity to change your minds?

Shadrach Oh yes. He first asked us if it was really true that we refused to serve his gods and to worship the golden image. I think he half-expected us to say it wasn't true!

DANIEL • STUDY 3 • OUR GOD IS ABLE • · · · ·

| Meshach | Then he offered us a second chance. He said that if we were willing to fall down and worship the image, he would overlook the past, and everything would be all right. |

| Abednego | I think he must have seen the calm, confident looks on our faces, for then he got angry and threatened us with death in the furnace if we refused to obey. |

| Shadrach | But his final appeal, to our reason and logic, actually strengthened our determination to stand firm. He asked us what god would be able to rescue us. |

| Meshach | That was a good opening for us, wasn't it? We gave him a direct answer. We said that our God, the God whom we served, was able to save us from the fire, and would rescue us from him. |

| Interviewer | But how could you be so sure? |

| Abednego | Well, you see, that's what faith is all about. It was by faith in our God that we were able to come out of the fire unscathed. |

| Interviewer | Ah, but didn't you admit there was a possibility that God wouldn't save you? |

| Meshach | It was like this. What God expected of us was that we should stand firm and refuse to bow down and worship the image. That was the important issue. After that, it was over to Him. It was for Him to decide whether to glorify His name by keeping us from harm, or to glorify it by letting us die the martyr's death. |

| Interviewer | That's a very brave way to look at life. |

| Shadrach | Our lives are in God's hands, and He has told us not to be afraid of those who kill the body but cannot kill the soul. Rather, we are to fear the One who can destroy both soul and body in the fires of hell. |

| Meshach | I'd like to put a question to our viewers: Where do you stand? Are you prepared to offer yourself completely to God, that He might be glorified in your body; or are you more concerned with holding on to your life at all costs? |

STUDY 4

A MAN WHO FOUND GOD

QUESTIONS

DAY 1   *Daniel 4:1-7. This chapter is a state document issued by a king.*
a) Who was meant to read it?

b) What was the king's purpose in writing it?

DAY 2   *Daniel 4:8-12, 22.*
a) When was Daniel called in to interpret the dream?

b) What is said about the tree?

c) How was the tree a picture of Nebuchadnezzar at that time?

DAY 3   *Daniel 4:13-18.*
a) Who spoke in the dream and what was said about the tree?

b) What title is given to God?

c) What did God want everyone to know about Him? What practical effect should this knowledge have on our lives?

DAY 4   *Daniel 4:19-23.*
a) What similarities exist between this story and the parable in Luke 12:16-21?

QUESTIONS (contd.)

b) What important difference is there?

DAY 5 *Daniel 4:24-27.*
a) In stating God's purpose for bringing about this disaster, what additional detail does Daniel add in verse 25 (Compare with v. 17)?

b) Read verse 27 again carefully and compare it with Isaiah 1:18. What is God's greatest desire?

DAY 6 *Daniel 4:28-33.*
a) What was Nebuchadnezzar like, twelve months after his terrifying dream? (Read Ps. 10:2-6.)

b) What words do we usually say at the end of the Lord's Prayer? How are they in stark contrast to what Nebuchadnezzar said in verse 30?

DAY 7 *Daniel 4:34-37, and look back to verses 2 and 3.*
a) Finally, after seven years of living like an animal, what did Nebuchadnezzar do? What results came from this?

b) Suggest a headline for a newspaper article on the events of this chapter.

NOTES

Let's take a look at this man, Nebuchadnezzar. From history, we discover:

* he was one of the greatest kings ever,
* he built more brick buildings than anyone had ever done,
* he planned and built the first city that would be thought great, even by today's standards, with its man-made mountain and hanging gardens of Babylon,
* he was an utter despot, a man of violent passions and moods, yet an intellectual one who loved culture.

HOW DID GOD DEAL WITH THIS MAN?
How could He hope to get through to a heathen king such as this?

1. First, He sent him to Jerusalem to take the king of Judah captive. God knew that Nebuchadnezzar would use his brains and bring back the pick of the people and the goods that he found there, thus bringing godly men to Babylon.
2. Then God brought under his very nose four young Hebrews who loved their Lord and showed him the difference the one true God could make in a man's life.
3. God stepped into his subconscious with a dream, and showed Nebuchadnezzar that He was a God to be reckoned with.
4. But Nebuchadnezzar was a hard man to convince, so next God permitted him to see a miracle, as He saved Shadrach, Meshach and Abednego from the fiery furnace. Now the king was ready to acknowledge Him – but only as another god, the god of the Hebrews.
5. God left him alone to think, and Nebuchadnezzar turned back to his gigantic building programme which would make Babylon the greatest city in the world.
6. But God wasn't finished with Nebuchadnezzar yet. He gave him another dream, which terrified him. And He pleaded with him, through His servant Daniel, to repent of his sin. But still Nebuchadnezzar thought he could do without God.
7. Twelve months later, tragedy struck. At the height of his self-made glory and pride, he lost his reason, and was brought down to the dust. For seven long years he lived like an animal, and THEN ... a completely changed Nebuchadnezzar got back his sanity, as he raised his eyes towards God and saw Him for who He is. He had found God!

Was God unkind? Was He unfair? Was He cruel to bring such suffering on a man? Let's ask Nebuchadnezzar himself.

After his ordeal, he says: 'I ... praise and exalt and glorify the king of heaven, – because **everything he does** is right'.
What is God saying to you in your circumstances?
Have you found Him for yourself yet?
Learn these words from verse 37 by heart, and make them your own:

'I praise and exalt and glorify the king of heaven, because **everything he does** is right.'

STUDY 5

THE NATION THAT LOST GOD

QUESTIONS

DAY 1 *Daniel 5:1-4; Exodus 40:9-11.*
a) Make a list of the evil things Belshazzar and his guests were doing in this passage.

b) I Corinthians 3:16-17. Discuss ways in which people deliberately profane holy things today.

DAY 2 *Daniel 5:4-6.*
a) What startled the king out of his drunken stupor?

b) How did he react to what he saw?

c) Find some similarities between this event and that described in I Thessalonians 5:2-3.

DAY 3 *Daniel 5:7-9.*
a) What did Belshazzar do as a reaction to the writing? What added to his turmoil (v. 9)?

b) Psalm 46:1-2; I Peter 5:7. What can the Christian do when trouble comes?

QUESTIONS (contd.)

DAY 4 *Daniel 5:10-16.*
a) What wise advice did the Queen Mother give to Belshazzar? Was she right in everything she said?

b) What do we find when we compare verse 14 with 4:8?

c) How do we know the king was not in the habit of consulting Daniel?

DAY 5 *Daniel 5:17-21.*
a) What aspects of the life of Nebuchadnezzar did Daniel summarise?

b) What parallel exists between what Daniel said and what Paul wrote in 1 Corinthians 10:6-11?

DAY 6 *Daniel 5:22-24; Romans 1:18-21.*
a) What did Daniel accuse Belshazzar of?

b) Is Romans 1:18-21 a commentary on Belshazzar's life? Is it describing us as well?

DAY 7 *Daniel 5:25-31.*
a) What message had God for Belshazzar and how soon was it fulfilled?

b) The three words remind us of some things God is saying to us today. Which word (MENE, TEKEL, PARSIN) would you associate with the following verses – Romans 6:23; Job 14:5; Romans 3:23?

NOTES

Who was Belshazzar?

His mother was one of Nebuchadnezzar's daughters. How vividly the story of her father's seven year madness would have been passed on to her son! Belshazzar grew up knowing exactly how the God of the Hebrews had dealt with his grandfather. But the warning fell on deaf ears, as the young man went his merry way.

Politically, the country had been through unsettled times. After Nebuchadnezzar's death one king was assassinated after only two years on the throne, another reigned for four years and a third was murdered after nine months. Then Belshazzar's father stepped in and usurped the throne and his young son became a prince overnight. As he grew to manhood Belshazzar made the most of the glittering empire that lay at his feet, and when his father became increasingly involved in military campaigns away from home he was more than delighted to be made co-regent. (Hence his offer to make Daniel the third highest ruler in the kingdom.)

Why was the nation no longer God-conscious?

In the space of some twenty years since Nebuchadnezzar's death, things had simply been allowed to slide.

* Daniel was no longer required, and was forgotten.
* The Queen Mother's influence was pushed aside.
* The nation felt it was doing very well without God.
* The king did not honour God, so why should anyone else?

How does our nation compare with this?

Could God say to us: 'You **knew**, but you did not honour the God who holds in His hand your life and all your ways?'

Remember the dream about the huge statue?

Babylon was the head of gold. But God, who 'sets up kings and deposes them' (2:21) had weighed the kingdom on the scales and found it wanting. The time for judgment had come, and the head of gold was to give way to the chest and arms of silver.

How was the kingdom overthrown?

Babylon was proud of its impregnable city, with its double walls of brick, 300 feet high and 85 feet broad, its 250 towers and its fortress which had a circuit of ten kilometres.

The city was built on both sides of the River Euphrates, and Cyrus, king of Persia devised a cunning plan. To divert the course of the river he secretly had a new channel dug, and then opened this new channel on the very night that the king and all his nobles, lulled into a false sense of security, were celebrating, in drunken revelry, a festival to their gods. The Persian army was able to march along the river bed under cover of darkness, under the city gates, and into the palace. We know what happened to Belshazzar.

And Darius the Mede?

Cyrus had absorbed Media into the Persian Empire. He now gave Darius charge of his new conquest.

Truly, 'the Most High God is sovereign over the kingdoms of men, and sets over them anyone he wishes' (Dan. 5:21).

STUDY 6

A MAN OF PRAYER

QUESTIONS

DAY 1 *Daniel 6:1-4.*

a) Why might these men have tried to bring charges against Daniel?

b) What parallel exists between Matthew 26:59-60 and this passage?

DAY 2 *Daniel 6:5-10.*

a) Why was the king asked to issue this special decree? What did it say and what did Daniel do?

b) What aspect of Daniel's prayer is noted?

c) Why is it so important for every Christian to have a regular, daily prayer times?

DAY 3 *Daniel 6:11-14.*

a) Another aspect of prayer is mentioned here. What is it?

b) Man-made laws can be bad. Can you think of any that are harmful today?

c) John 19:4-12. What had Darius and Pilate in common?

QUESTIONS (contd.)

DAY 4   *Daniel 6:15-18; Matthew 27:57-66.*
a) What had impressed Darius about Daniel? What did he think of Daniel's God (see also v. 20).

b) What similarities can you find between verse 17 and the 'Matthew' reading?

DAY 5   *Daniel 6:19-22.*
a) When did the king return to the den? What suggests he was eager to find out what had happened?

b) What had Daniel in common with Peter in Acts 12:6-11?

DAY 6   *Daniel 6:23-24; John 20:25-27.*
a) What difference is shown here between Daniel after his ordeal and Jesus after His resurrection?

b) How does verse 24 prove that Daniel's escape was miraculous?

DAY 7   *Daniel 6:25-28; Revelation 1:18.*
a) What description of God by King Darius is taken up by the Lord Jesus in Revelation 1:18?

b) How was Genesis 50:20 true in Daniel's life?

NOTES

What can we find in this well-known story to help us in our daily lives?

Daniel lived a life of trust in God.
He was probably over ninety years of age at the time we are reading about!

Everything we know about him underlines his complete trust in God. Nothing diverted him from doing what God wanted, and even his enemies could find nothing of which they could accuse him.

God says to us, 'Be holy, because I am holy' (I Pet. 1:16).

He had three spiritual meals a day.
Talking with God was vital to Daniel. How else could he keep his spirit strong in a land where few people loved God? His habit of regular prayer times is one that we can copy. We may need to give up something else but we need to get our priorities right. Daniel may sometimes have felt prayer was hard work (10:8) but he persevered.

God tells us to 'pray continually' (I Thess. 5:17).

In a time of crisis God delivered him.
Why? It was because his daily walk with the Lord kept him right in the centre of God's will. For ninety years he had put God first, been obedient to Him, and learned to trust Him in every situation. I'm sure he knew God could handle this one too! Are you preparing in the same way for any crisis which might come to you? Paul tells how, at his trial in Rome, all his friends deserted him. 'But,' he says 'the Lord stood at my side, and I was delivered from the lion's mouth. The Lord will rescue me from every evil attack, and will bring me safely to His heavenly kingdom' (2 Tim. 4:17-18).

God says to us, 'Those who honour me, I will honour' (I Sam. 2:30).

STUDY 7

WHAT IS THE WORLD COMING TO?

QUESTIONS

Chapters 1–6 are historical facts, recorded after they had taken place. *Chapters 7–12* tell of Daniel's prophetic dreams and visions, written in symbolic language.

DAY 1 *Daniel 7:1-3, 17; Isaiah 57:20-21.*
a) What did Daniel notice first in his dream?

b) How are the beasts compared and contrasted in verse 3?

c) What do the beasts represent?

DAY 2 *Daniel 7:4-8.*
a) What did each beast look like?

b) What do you notice when you compare these beasts with the one beast mentioned in Revelation 13:1-2?

DAY 3 *Daniel 7:9-12.*
a) Try to picture the scene described here. What impresses you the most about it? Who is the focus of attention?

b) What is the significance of God being called the 'Ancient of Days' (v. 9)?

QUESTIONS (contd.)

DAY 4 *Daniel 7:13-14.*
a) What is said about the 'one like a son of man' (v. 13)?

b) Jesus frequently used the title, 'Son of Man', of Himself. In the light of this 'Daniel' passage why might he have done so? (A possible clue is to consider the effect that Jesus' words in Matt. 26:63-65 had on the High Priest.)

DAY 5 *Daniel 7:15-18.*
a) Who will receive the Kingdom and possess it for ever?

b) Who are described as saints in the New Testament (Eph. 1:1, 13; Phil. 1:1)?

DAY 6 *Daniel 7:19-26.*
a) What can you discover about the little horn, or apparent final world ruler?

b) How will the power of this person be brought to an end?

DAY 7 *Daniel 7:27-28; Revelation 11:15.*
a) What do these passages have in common?

b) Do you feel as Daniel did in verse 28? Why, or why not?

NOTES

When you stop to think of the kind of world in which your children and grandchildren will grow up, do you become alarmed and pessimistic? The present unrest and terrorism in so many countries, the threat of nuclear war, declining moral standards, famine and starvation in the Third World ... do these things concern you? They certainly should concern us, but, as Christians, we should not lose sight of the ultimate hope.

As Belshazzar the Playboy Prince came to the throne, Daniel felt the same kind of insecurity that we sometimes feel, so God comforted and reassured him with his dream.

He showed him that:

a) The Most High God is, always was, and always will be in control of His world.

b) Evil, though terrifyingly real and powerful, has a limited time before it is destroyed.

c) The 'saints of the Most High' (believers) will one day reign with Jesus forever.

The few short years of our life span will seem as nothing compared with eternity. Peter asks: 'What kind of people ought you to be?' and answers: 'You ought to live holy and godly lives, as you look forward to the day of God.... So then, dear friends, since you are looking forward to this, make every effort to be found spotless, blameless, and at peace with Him' (2 Pet. 3:11-14).

If your friends say to you: 'Look what the world is coming to!' you can reply: 'Ah, but look who has come to the world' – and you can share Jesus with them.

STUDY 8

GOD ALLOWS A GLIMPSE INTO THE FUTURE

QUESTIONS

DAY 1 *Daniel 8:1-4; 5:30, 31.*

The symbols of this vision were explained to Daniel *before* the events took place, but as we look *back* in history, we can see them being vividly fulfilled.

a) Of what country was Belshazzar king?

b) Describe the appearance of the first animal mentioned. What did it do?

DAY 2 *Daniel 8:5-8, 21-22.*

a) How is the advance of the goat from the west described?

b) Alexander the Great was the first king of Greece. On his death his kingdom was divided among four generals. How does this vision represent this? Try to find out more from history books if possible.

DAY 3 *Daniel 8:9-12, 23.*

a) What do these verses in Daniel tell us about the next world ruler? A person called Antiochus fulfilled this to the letter.

b) Why do you think God allowed these atrocities to happen (Isaiah 1:4)?

QUESTIONS (contd.)

DAY 4 *Daniel 8:13-14.*
a) How do we know from these two verses, that God was still in control?

b) What aspect of the vision were the angels concerned about?

DAY 5 *Daniel 8:15-18.*
a) What was Daniel's reaction to seeing the heavenly messenger?

b) The angel Gabriel is mentioned only on two other occasions in the Bible

(Luke 1:13, 19, 26-33). To whom did he appear and what messages did he bring?

DAY 6 *Daniel 8:19-25.*
a) What is again emphasised about the wicked king in verse 25?

b) Some think that the reference to the end (vv. 17, 19) may also refer to a later period than that of Antiochus? With help from Matthew 24:10-16, 29-31 to what period might they be referring to?

DAY 7 *Daniel 8:26, 27; John 16:13-15.*
a) What final details are given concerning the vision?

b) Why might Daniel have reacted the way he did to the vision?

NOTES

The Bible says, 'Everything written in the Scriptures was written to teach us' (Rom. 15:4, GNB).

What can we learn from Alexander the Great?
Standing back, as we do today some 2,300 years later, what do we see? We see a man with high ambition, dogged determination, incredible energy and perseverance. His goal – to conquer the world. And he achieved that goal ... but at what cost!

How often men or women put everything they have got into getting to the top, in academic, business, political or social life, only to find that in the process their health or perhaps their family relationships, have crumbled. Having conquered, they find they have defeated themselves, through their colossal expenditure of effort to win.

Alexander, can we learn from you to keep a balance in our lives? To aim for the highest, yes, but not at the expense of things which are, perhaps, more precious than we realize?

Jesus said, 'Does a man gain anything if he wins the whole world but loses his life?'

What can we learn from Antiochus?
The 'monstrous outrages' that this king inflicted on the Jews have been set down for all time in the Apocrypha, in 1 Maccabees chapter 1 and 2 Maccabees chapters 6 and 7. They make chilling reading. Yet, from what the angel said to Daniel, we can see that he was a type of the final antichrist who will one day hold world power.

The reason Antiochus gained the confidence of the people in Jerusalem to begin with was that they had gradually become less like the people of God and more like the other nations. When the Greek ruler marched into the Holy City he found a people who had already adopted Greek culture and philosophy, who were enjoying Greek entertainment, and who even dressed like the Greeks. They had let slide the moral standards their God had given them.

What can we learn from this? On every side, Christians are being urged to be like everyone else, to conform to peer pressure – while our Lord Jesus still says to His people: 'Therefore come out from them and be separate ... Touch no unclean thing, and I will receive you' (2 Cor. 6:17).

What can we learn from Daniel?
The dreadful events he saw in his vision literally made him sick. And he looked around at the Jews, almost submerged in Babylonian culture, and felt sick with apprehension.

Are you concerned – really concerned – with those around you who don't know the Lord, who are going to a Christless eternity?

But did you notice one short sentence in verse 27? 'Then I got up and went about the king's business.' Nothing should divert us from going about THE KING'S business, sharing the Good News with others, so that we can present ourselves to God as workmen who do 'not need to be ashamed' (2 Tim. 2:15).

STUDY 9

ANSWERED PRAYER

QUESTIONS

DAY 1 *Daniel 9:1-3; Jeremiah 25:1, 8-11; Jeremiah 29:10-14.*
a) What must Daniel have been reading at this time?

b) After his Bible Study, what did he do? How do we know that he was being earnest in this?

DAY 2 *Daniel 9:4-6.*
a) What had God promised in 2 Chronicles 7:13-14?

b) What indications are there that the people had not been calling upon God?

DAY 3 *Daniel 9:4-10.*
a) Make two lists: one list should contain what Daniel declares about God, the other, his description of his nation.

b) Why might the word 'we' in verse 5 surprise you (see also v. 20)?

DAY 4 *Daniel 9:11-14.*
a) Why did Daniel not complain to God about all the trouble the nation was experiencing?

b) Hebrews 2:1-3. Why should we take the warning in verse 3 seriously?

QUESTIONS (contd.)

DAY 5 *Daniel 9:15-19; Nehemiah 1:5-7.*
a) On what grounds did Daniel present his petitions?

b) In what way was Nehemiah's prayer similar to that of Daniel'?

DAY 6 *Daniel 9:20-23; Isaiah 43:1.*
a) Why did Gabriel come to Daniel

b) As well as an answer to prayer, what else was Daniel assured of through Gabriel?

DAY 7 *Daniel 9:24-27. These verses have been interpreted in various ways, and you should refer to a commentary if you have queries.*
a) What can you discover about the Anointed One (God's chosen leader)?

b) What tragic happenings are forecast? But how does the prophecy end?

NOTES

Have you ever made a study of actual prayers of great men in the Bible? You might like to. Here are a few to start with:

Abraham: Genesis 18:22-33.
Moses: Exodus 32:31, 32; 33:12-13.
Elijah: I Kings 18:36, 37.
David: Psalm 51:1-12.
Early Christians: Acts 4:24-30.
Paul: Ephesians 3:14-21.

This is an effective way of deepening your own prayer life.

And in our study this week, we see Daniel in prayer. Three times a day he knelt at his open window and talked with God.

What was the basis for his prayer?

We have seen that Bible Study was, for him, an encounter with the living God. As exiles in a foreign land the Jews had been careful to bring with them the scrolls of Moses' writings and the prophets. They would have spent time copying them out and sharing them around. The very phrases Daniel used in the prayer we have been studying echo the words so often used in the earlier Scriptures:

e.g. 'O Lord ... who keeps his covenant of love.'
'We have turned away from your commands and laws.'
'O Lord our God, who brought your people out of Egypt.'

When you talk to God do you base your prayers on what He has been saying to you through His word?

What was the reason for his prayer?

First, a promise. God had promised that after seventy years He would bring His people back to their land. Now Daniel claims that promise.

Do you claim God's promises when you pray? Promises like: 'If any of you lacks wisdom, he should ask God, who gives generously' (Jas. 1:5); 'in all your ways acknowledge him and he will make your paths straight' (Prov. 3:6).

Then, a need. And Daniel knew he had to confess sin with utter sincerity before he could make his requests for the nation. This is something we can learn to do, both on a national and on a personal level.

What was the answer to his prayer?

A bit disappointing, perhaps? God gave him a wider view of the situation. Yes, He would bring His people back, but this would not cure their sin. It would not be the answer to their basic problems.

Sometimes we pray for physical healing, or for a happy outcome to a situation. But God has a wider view, and His purpose is to bring people close to Himself so that they will put Him first in their lives. He desires our holiness most of all, even before our happiness here on earth.

Yet God had the Perfect Answer in store whereby the people's sin could be perfectly atoned for and forgiven, and again He allows Daniel a glimpse into the future. Remember that Jesus Himself is the answer to our problems. He doesn't just give us peace – He is our peace. He doesn't just make us loving – He is love, and He can dwell in us.

So … don't forget what we have learned in this study! Put into practice what the Lord has been saying to you. 'Do not merely listen to the word … Do what it says (Jas. 1:22).

STUDY 10

SPIRITUAL WARFARE

QUESTIONS

DAY 1 *Daniel 10:1-3; 9:25.*
a) When was Daniel given this revelation? What had happened two years earlier in Cyrus' reign (Ezra 1:1-3)?

b) What kind of message was Daniel about to be given?

DAY 2 *Daniel 10:4-6; Revelation 1:12-16.*
a) The exact identity of the figure Daniel saw is left vague but comparing it with the vision in Revelation, what can we assume?

b) What similarities are there in these two visions?

DAY 3 *Daniel 10:7-11; Acts 9:3-7.*
a) How did Daniel's friends and the men travelling with Paul react to the vision described in each passage?

b) What was Daniel's reaction? How was he reassured?

DAY 4 *Daniel 10:12-13. Look back to verse 2.*
a) How long had Daniel been fasting and praying for?

b) When had his prayer been heard?

QUESTIONS (contd.)

c) How long had the Heavenly Person been on his way? What does this tell us about answers to our prayers?

DAY 5 *Daniel 10:12-13,20; 12:1.*
a) The term 'prince' (NIV) here refers to a spiritual being, evil or good.

Why had Daniel to wait for an answer to his prayer?

b) Who was Michael and what did he do?

c) John 12:31; Ephesians 6:11-18. What do these verses teach us about spiritual warfare?

DAY 6 *Daniel 10:14-19.*
a) Why had the heavenly visitor come?

b) Jeremiah 1:4-9. In what way was Daniel's experience similar to that of Jeremiah?

c) Who can we depend on to help us speak out for God (Acts 1:8)?

DAY 7 *Daniel 10:20-21; 11:1.*
a) With whom would the heavenly visitor engage in spiritual warfare next?

b) What special book is referred to here and what might it be (Ps. 139:16)?

NOTES

'Look at that old man over there! Eighty-six years old, if he's a day. Look at him, sitting on the bank of the river, his hair unkempt, his beard growing shaggy, and – oh! there's rather an unpleasant smell coming from him as if he hasn't washed for weeks. And how gaunt he looks! Let's go over and speak to him.'

'Excuse me ... I seem to recognise you, but I'm not sure. Are you – er – Daniel, the man greatly beloved by God?'

'Yes, indeed, I am Daniel.'

'Well, it's Passover Time – don't you know? The time when your people are celebrating the deliverance from Egypt. Yet obviously you aren't joining with them.'

'No, my friend. I have been mourning, fasting and praying for three weeks now.'

'Mourning? But why? Only two years ago King Cyrus allowed your people to return and rebuild Jerusalem. Fifty thousand of them have gone back – isn't that a tremendous answer to prayer?'

'Fifty thousand! Yes, and what about the many thousands more who did not want to return? The Lord has shown me I must remain here and pray. My brethren are so settled in this foreign culture that they don't want the blessings God is offering to them.'

'Oh, I see. But the faithful ones who went, can't you be happy about them?'

'Faithful? That's just it. Their enthusiasm has waned. The walls are still in ruins and, moreover, the people are fighting among themselves. God's people in God's land, grabbing for themselves at the expense of their brothers. Oh, what sin and wickedness!

I must fast and pray, and plead with God Almighty for my nation. For seventy years the people have waited and said, "When the Lord brings back the captives to Jerusalem, our mouths will be filled with laughter and our tongues with songs of joy" ... but it has not been so. It is not deliverance from Babylon that brings joy, it is **obedience** to the laws of our God. And my people are still refusing to obey Him.

Daniel had a problem	... God had the answer.
Daniel humbled himself before the Lord and prayed for understanding	... God heard him from the very first day.
Daniel collapsed on the ground	... the 'man' raised him up.
Daniel became speechless	... the 'man' made him able to speak.
Daniel was weak and breathless	... the 'man' made him strong.

Can you identify with Daniel in any of these areas? If you can, then this week's study will help you to remember that God can meet every need. If you are in the centre of His will, as Daniel was, He can enable you to stand firm, give you His words to speak, and make you strong. He tells you to be strong in the Lord, and in His mighty power.

STUDY 11

HISTORY LESSON ... IN ADVANCE

QUESTIONS and NOTES

History books may seem dull and boring, but when we can hold the Bible in one hand and the events of history in the other, we are fascinated and amazed. Listed below are facts of history which took place between the years 530 BC and 164 BC. Daniel wrote down the things recorded here, in 537 BC, before any of them happened.

The Good News Bible is not the most helpful for this study which will be done rather differently from usual.

DAYS 1, 2, 3: Carefully compare the Bible verses with the historical facts. Then write the corresponding verse number at the right hand side.

DAYS 4, 5: Compare again, and answer the questions.

DAYS 6, 7: Think, pray, discuss, and write down your answers.

DAY 1 *Daniel 11:2-4.*

530 BC	Cyrus, King of Persia, died. Three kings reigned after him.
485-465 BC	King Xerxes of Persia came to the throne. Noted for his great wealth. Invaded Greece, but was defeated. Verse ....
465-336 BC	Persia, no longer a world power, had seven minor kings in succession.
336 BC	Alexander the Great ruled Greece and conquered Persia – see Study 8. Verse ....
323 BC	At his death the vast empire was divided between four generals as his two sons had been murdered. Verse ....

42

QUESTIONS and NOTES (contd.)

Two of these generals increased in power –
Seleucus in Syria, **north** of Israel; and Ptolemy in Egypt, **south** of Israel. These two dynasties continued under a succession of kings until 65 BC and 30 BC respectively.

To simplify these notes, we shall refer to the various kings who ruled these countries over that period of almost 300 years as 'the king of Syria' and 'the king of Egypt' though you can find out their rather complicated names from any history book of the period.

DAY 2   *Daniel 11:5-9.*
       323 BC   Ptolemy became king of Egypt.
       312 BC   Seleucus formed his own kingdom of Syria.
                                      Verse ....

       248 BC   The king of Egypt gave his daughter Berenice in marriage to the king of Syria in an attempt to make peace. For this the king of Syria had to divorce his wife Laodice, who subsequently murdered him and poisoned Berenice and her children. Her father also died.   Verse ....

       244 BC   Berenice's brother, now king of Egypt, attacked Syria to avenge his sister's murder. He put Laodice to death,
                                        Verse ....
              and returned triumphant with much wealth and booty.
                                        Verse ....

       240 BC   The king of Syria returned the attack but was defeated.
                                      Verse ....

Verses 10-15 describe the many wars between Egypt and Syria with every detail exactly true to history.

QUESTIONS and NOTES (contd.)

DAY 3 *Daniel 11:16-20.*

223 BC   Antiochus the Great, king of Syria, was completely successful in all his campaigns against the Egyptian forces. He then occupied Israel. Verse ....

194 BC   He gave his daughter Cleopatra to the king of Egypt in marriage in the hope that Egypt would ally with him against the newly-emerging world power – Rome. However, Cleopatra sided with her husband against her father. Verse ....

193-187 BC Antiochos the Great went to war against the Romans capturing many islands in the Mediterranean, but it proved to be his last campaign. A Roman commander defeated him, he returned home, and was killed by his countrymen. Verse ....

187 BC   His son, the new king of Syria, raised taxes, and sent his prime minister to seize funds of the Temple treasury in Jerusalem. This man eventually poisoned the king. Verse ....

DAY 4 *Daniel 11:21-30(a).*

175 BC   Antiochus Epiphanes usurped the throne of Syria. This is the man mentioned in 8:23-25 (see Study 8). a) What can you find out about his character from verses 21-24?

170 BC   Invasion of Egypt. Antiochus had an overwhelming victory, and returned with much wealth.

168 BC   Second campaign against Egypt. His purpose was to take the entire nation of Egypt and make it part of his empire. But Rome sent ships to help Egypt, and Antiochus withdrew.

b) What is the significance of the words 'at the appointed time' (vv. 27, 29)?

DAY 5 *Daniel 11:30(b)-35.*

168 BC   After Antiochus had invaded Jerusalem and taken it, he ordered the sanctuary to be polluted and sacrifice and worship to cease (I Maccabees 1:37-49).
a) What two kinds of people (among the Jews) are referred to in verse 32?

b) What is prophesied for God's people?

DAY 6 a) Look at a map to find out where Israel is in relation to Syria and Egypt. How would these centuries of wars have affected Israel?

b) Why do you think God so carefully preserved this tiny nation (Gen. 12:2-3; Isa. 9:2, 6-7)?

DAY 7 Think back over the study again.
a) What does it show us about God?

b) What does it show us about men of power (see vv. 3, 16, 36)?

STUDY 12

DANIEL WILL BE THERE – WILL YOU?

QUESTIONS

DAY 1 *Daniel 11:36-39.*
a) What major sin characterizes this figure?

b) Some of these predictions are true about Antiochus Epiphanes, but not all. Whom does he foreshadow (1 John 2:22)?

DAY 2 *Daniel 11:40-45.*
a) To what period of time does the prophecy now shift (see beginning of v. 40)?

b) Many think verse 45 refers to the battle of Armageddon (Rev. 16:14-16; 19:19-20). Who will have the final victory?

DAY 3 *Daniel 12:1.*
a) What all is said about 'your people' (NIV)?

b) Matthew 24:21-22, 29-30. What happens in these verses?

DAY 4 *Daniel 12:2-4; Matthew 13:36-43; 25:46.*
(Note that 'sleep' in the Bible is used of the body, never the soul.)
a) What are the only two divisions of mankind that God recognises?

b) How can you be sure which group you will be in (1 John 5:11-12)?

QUESTIONS (contd.)

DAY 5 *Daniel 12:5-9.*
a) If you were drawing a picture of the events of these verses, who would be in it (compare several versions)?

b) How are these end time events described in verse 6?

c) What kind of an answer did Daniel get to his question?

DAY 6 *Daniel 12:9-12.*
a) Because you are now reading this prophecy, what can you conclude about our day and age (v. 9; Rev. 16:15)?

b) Various attempts have been made to calculate dates from these verses. What did Jesus say about this in Matthew 24:36?

DAY 7 *Daniel 12:13; Job 19:26; Isaiah 26:19.*
Only rarely in the Old Testament do we find references to the resurrection of the body. Yet what is the Christian's assurance, as shown in I Corinthians 15:20-23 and I Peter 1:3-5?

NOTES

What impressions have you gained from your study of the book of Daniel? Can you remember what is the main message of this book?

See how God was in complete control of everything that happened to Daniel, from the time when he was taken captive as a young man to the very end of his long life.

If you love the Lord and are true to Him be assured that He will also control the events that come into your life. Are you willing to trust Him as far as Daniel did? (Remember Study 6?) Do you have the assurance that what is happening in the world today is under God's control? It may not seem like it at times, but we can be sure that God is working His purposes out and that nothing takes Him by surprise.

As you study God's word you will become more and more convinced that He is in complete control of the time towards which history is moving – 'the end time'. As the song says:

'I know not what the future holds,
But I know who holds the future.'

Do you personally know the One who holds the future? Daniel did, and his Lord showed him that he was 'highly esteemed'. And we, who have heard the Good News of Jesus Christ, will have no excuse on the Day of Judgment if we have not, before then, given ourselves to Him and asked Him to take complete control of our lives.

In the heavenly Jerusalem the Lord God Almighty will reign. Those who have been wise and led others to righteousness will shine like the brightness of the heavens and like the stars for ever and ever.

Daniel will be there, and many others whose names are familiar to us from our Bible Studies. All those who love the Lord and have put Him first during their lives on earth will rejoice together at the Wedding Feast of the Lamb, that is, the Lord Jesus.

Yes, Daniel will be there ... will you?

ANSWER GUIDE

The following pages contain an Answer Guide. It is recommended that answers to the questions be attempted before turning to this guide. It is only a guide and the answers given should not be treated as exhaustive.

GUIDE TO STUDY 1

DAY 1   a) God allowed it to happen. (Jehoiakim was evil, and had led the people away from God.) People and items from the temple were taken away to Babylon.
b) More items from the temple and people were taken away. The temple was finally set on fire.

DAY 2   a) They were members either of the royal family or the nobility .
b) Because of their background, handsome appearance and academic ability.

DAY 3   a) It was a three-year humanities course in the Babylonian language.
b) Make them forget about the true God, and identify with the Babylonian culture.

DAY 4   a) He did not want to be defiled by the royal food and wine.
b) Daniel must have viewed that taking the royal food and wine implied participation in the idolatrous worship of the king.

DAY 5   a) He asked for permission to refuse the food and wine; he suggested an alternative and proposed a ten day test period.
b) He was respectful, polite, wise, persistent and was confident that he was doing right.

DAY 6   a) God honoured Daniel's stand by intervening and causing the official in charge to show him favour and sympathy.
Sometimes we may feel frightened of doing something we know we should do. When we do it we find that God goes before and helps us.
b) Personal.
c) At the end of the ten days they were looking healthier than those who had eaten the royal food.

DAY 7   a) God gave them superior mental knowledge and understanding; to Daniel he gave spiritual gifts.
b) They would realise that God was still with them and working among those who were being faithful to him in Babylon. He could intervene in seemingly impossible situations.

GUIDE TO STUDY 2

DAY 1 a) He was troubled by the dream he had had and the failure of his advisors to interpret it.
The inability of those around him to tell him what he had dreamed.
b) What he had asked was beyond human ability ; only 'the gods' could help him.

DAY 2 a) He was under threat of death.
b) He spoke tactfully to Arioch; he obtained a stay of execution; he urged his friends to pray for an understanding of Nebuchadnezzar's dream.
c) We should share our problems with others and encourage them to pray; we need to realise that it is only because of God's mercy that He answers us; we need to trust Him completely to show us a way through our problems.

DAY 3 a) He revealed the dream and its meaning to Daniel in a night vision.
b) He immediately began to praise and thank God.
God is wise and powerful. He is in control of history and gives wisdom and revelation. He dwells in light and He had answered their specific prayer request.

DAY 4 a) As a God in heaven who reveals mysteries. Daniel refused to take any credit for the explanation he was about to give.
b) He said the dream would reveal to the king future world events.

DAY 5 a) Gold. Silver. Bronze.
b) Iron. Iron and clay.
c) The value decreases, the brilliance decreases, they get harder as they go down; the feet are the weakest and when hit there the whole structure falls.

DAY 6 a) Cut out of a mountain but not by human hands. It breaks and brings to an end all other kingdoms.
b) They clearly identity the Lord Jesus as the 'stone'. Though rejected He clearly is the most important stone; anyone opposing Him will be crushed.

DAY 7 a) God is greater than any other god; He has authority over kings; He reveals mysteries.
b) He was made ruler over the whole of Babylon and put in charge of all its wise men.
c) That Shadrach, Meshach and Abednego become administrators.

GUIDE TO STUDY 3

DAY 1 a) To worship the image he had set up.
b) Everybody would be doing it; there was a threat of death for refusing to worship the image; music can sway emotions.

DAY 2 a) Three Jews: Shadrach, Meshach and Abednego.
b) Perhaps they were jealous of these men as the king had put them in important positions (Dan. 1:20; 2:49).

DAY 3 a) He imagined himself equal or even superior to the power of any god.
b) They declared their assurance that God was able to rescue them.
c) They have the help of the Holy Spirit to teach them what to say.

DAY 4 a) – our God is able to save us,
   – He will rescue us,
   – but even if He does not,
   – we will not serve your gods.
b) Personal.

DAY 5 a) He ordered the furnace to be heated more, and he had the Hebrews bound with ropes and thrown in.
b) He saw four men in the fire; they were unbound (had the fire burned the ropes?); and they were unhurt.

DAY 6 a) All the important people of the land.
b) Suggestions: to glorify His name (v. 26), to appeal again to the king to serve Him; yet remember that God's purposes are sometimes furthered by death, e.g. Jesus.

DAY 7 a) That He was unique and He had rescued His servants.
b) That they had trusted in God , preferring to put Him first in their lives rather than be swayed by the threats against them. Compare the 'Revelation' reading.
c) Personal.

GUIDE TO STUDY 4

DAY 1 a) Everyone in the known world.
b) That everyone might hear about what God had done for him.

DAY 2 a) When those who had been called in (v. 7) failed to interpret the dream.
b) It was large and strong, visible over all the earth. It had beautiful leaves, abundant fruit, and shelter and provision for every living creature.
c) He was great and powerful, flourishing, the head of a kingdom which extended far and wide.

DAY 3 a) A 'messenger' from heaven spoke. The tree was to be cut down with only the stump and roots to remain; the animals and birds would flee from it.
b) Most translations have Most High.
c) That He is sovereign over the kingdoms of men, and gives them to anyone He wishes.
Personal.

DAY 4 a) He was alarmed, perplexed and speechless. Perhaps he was shocked to realise the drastic measures God was going to take to bring the king to Himself.
b) Both men were rich and had no time for God, and God had to deal severely with both. Unlike Nebuchadnezzar, the rich fool had no opportunity to repent.

DAY 5 a) Nebuchadnezzar in particular is mentioned as requiring to acknowledge that God alone is sovereign even over human kings.
b) That people should come to Him as individuals, confessing their sins, so that He can forgive them and make them right in His sight.

DAY 6 a) Boastful, proud and unconcerned about God.
b) 'For Thine (Yours) is the kingdom, the power and the glory.'
Nebuchadnezzar said, 'For MINE is the kingdom, the power and the glory!'

DAY 7 a) He raised his eyes to heaven (animals don't do this). His sanity was restored; he praised and honoured God; his kingdom was returned to him; he became even greater than before.
b) Personal.

GUIDE TO STUDY 5

DAY 1 a) Drinking wine to excess; committing sacrilege with the vessels from the temple; praising idols.
b) Personal. Examples could include the misuse of their bodies through drug and sexual abuse; parodies on television on the life of Jesus or the Last Supper.

DAY 2 a) The fingers writing on the wall.
b) With great fear; he became weak and appeared almost to faint.
c) The coming again of the Lord Jesus will be sudden and unexpected for some. Those unprepared will be judged.

DAY 3 a) He called in his magicians, astrologers and diviners whom he thought could interpret the dream.
b) A Christian can turn to the Lord, casting every care on Him.

DAY 4 a) To call in Daniel.
No; Belshazzar had every right to be alarmed.
b) Nebuchadnezzar's description of him was repeated.
c) Daniel appears a foreigner to him in verse 13.

DAY 5 a) God had given Nebuchadnezzar everything he possessed. Through pride he temporarily lost power and only later recovered it when he acknowledged God as sovereign.
b) We are to learn and act upon the lessons we learn from history; they are more than stories to be remembered.

DAY 6 a) Instead of humbling himself before God and honouring Him, he had deliberately provoked God by drinking from the sacred vessels and worshipping idols.
b) Yes; Belshazzar is an example of someone who deliberately rejects true knowledge and becomes increasingly wicked.
Personal.

DAY 7 a) His reign was to end and his kingdom given to others.
That very night.
b) Mene – Job 14:5 (God knows how long our lives will be and we must be ready).
Tekel – Romans 3:23 (we are not up to God's standard).
Peres– Romans 6:23 (there is the choice of two destinies).

GUIDE TO STUDY 6

DAY 1 a) Daniel had been promoted over them; he no doubt refused to join in their corrupt practices; he was a Jew, and was devoted to his God.
b) People were looking for grounds on which to bring charges against both Daniel and the Lord Jesus, and both sets of people were initially unsuccessful.

DAY 2 a) The men were attempting to get rid of Daniel on religious grounds. No one was to pray to any god or man, except to the king, for thirty days. Daniel went home and prayed as usual to God.
b) Daniel gave thanks to God.
c) Suggestions: God is our Father and wants us to talk to Him; making it a habit makes it easier to remember; prayer is spiritual food, and we need it to keep up our spiritual strength; etc.

DAY 3 a) Specifically asking God for help.
b) Personal.
c) Both wanted the release of a victim they knew was innocent, but both were too weak to do what was right.

DAY 4 a) That he served his God continually (loyally). He obviously thought God might be able to save Daniel.
b) A stone was placed over the entrance, and sealed to prevent it from being moved.

DAY 5 a) At the first light of dawn. He hurried and went himself.
b) In both situations God used an angel to bring deliverance.

DAY 6 a) Daniel had no wounds (and had not suffered death), whereas Jesus was wounded for our sins.
b) The lions were hungry and immediately devoured the other people. Only God could have prevented them from tearing Daniel to pieces.

DAY 7 a) God is a 'living God', alive for ever and ever.
b) Though evil men had intended to harm Daniel, his deliverance resulted in all the nations being taught about the one true God and what He had done.

GUIDE TO STUDY 7

DAY 1
a) The wind churning up the sea.
b) Each was great and came up out of the sea, but each one was different.
c) Four kingdoms that would rise from the earth.

DAY 2
a) Like an animal: a lion, bear and leopard. The likeness of the fourth beast is not stated.
b) The beast described in Revelation 13 has the characteristics of all four.

DAY 3
a) Personal.
God.
b) 'Ancient' signifies that He always existed, and also that He is wise, full of understanding and experience.

DAY 4
a) He was given authority, glory and power; peoples and nations of every language worshipped Him.
b) It drew attention to His humanity, and yet was linked to deity through the 'Daniel' passage.

DAY 5
a) The saints of the Most High (people of the Supreme God).
b) Christians (believers).

DAY 6
a) He has eyes like a man with a loud bragging mouth; he wages war against God's people and defeats them; he defies God; tries to change laws and morals.
b) The heavenly court will sit in judgment; God will completely destroy him for ever.

DAY 7
a) The eternal nature of God's reign with everyone being subject to Him.
b) Personal. (Christians may not understand everything about the future but they should not feel as Daniel did because they belong to Christ who will triumph.)

Next week we shall be referring to the Apocrypha. The "Apocrypha" is the name given to fourteen books which originated in the period between the Old and New Testaments. Two of the books, 1 & 2 Maccabees, give accounts of the Jewish revolt against Antiochus Epiphanes and his immediate successors between 175 and 134 BC. You would find it helpful to read about the Apocrypha in such books as *The Lion Handbook to the Bible.*

GUIDE TO STUDY 8

It is helpful for you to have some information about the Apocrypha, as suggested last week.

DAY 1 a) Babylon.
b) A ram with two horns, one of which grew longer.
It did as it pleased charging west, north and south; it became great.
(Note that Persia was in the east of the known world, and lasted 200 years. It superseded Media).

DAY 2 a) As fast and furious (Alexander the Great became king at twenty-one, winning victory after victory over the Persians after attacking at breathtaking speed (v. 5) in a brilliant series of battles. With ever increasing momentum he went as far as India, until he wept because there were 'no more worlds to conquer').
b) As four horns replacing a large horn.

DAY 3 a) He would reach the south (Egypt), east (Persia) and the Beautiful Land (Palestine). He would devastate the temple, and be vicious and deceitful.
b) The Jews had turned their backs on God and indulged in sin. (I Maccabees 1:11-15 makes reference to the sports stadium where Jews, adopting Greek culture, competed naked, and sought to remove the marks of their circumcision.)

DAY 4 a) God had a time limit on Antiochus. (He began his oppression in 171 BC and 2,300 days later Judas Maccabaeus cleansed the temple.)
b) How long it would take before the vision would be fulfilled.

DAY 5 a) He was afraid and fell down with his face to the ground.
b) To Zechariah – that his elderly wife would have a son; and Mary – that she would bear the Son of God.

DAY 6 a) His deceit.
b) To the last days before Jesus returns.

DAY 7 a) It referred to a future period.
b) He may have been disturbed by the suffering that still lay ahead in the future.

GUIDE TO STUDY 9

DAY 1 a) The sacred books (Scriptures) and specifically the book of Jeremiah.
b) He prayed. He fasted and wore sackcloth and ashes.

DAY 2 a) Forgiveness and healing for the land if the people repented and sought Him again.
b) The people were ignoring His servants the prophets.

DAY 3 a) God: great and awesome; keeps His covenant of love; righteous; merciful and forgiving.
Nation: sinned and rebelled; turned from God; did not listen to prophets; covered with shame.
b) Though Daniel was a righteous man and highly esteemed by God, he still included himself in his own nation's sin.

DAY 4 a) The people were at fault in disobeying God. Daniel acknowledged that God is righteous in everything He does.
b) Just as a righteous God has punished in the past, so we may expect Him to fulfil His word today.

DAY 5 a) He appealed to God's mighty acts in the past (v. 15) and His great mercy (v. 18); he ask God to act for His own sake (vv. 17, 19) and because the city and people bore His name.
b) Both acknowledge who God is; both identify with their own nation and confess their own sins along with those of the people.

DAY 6 a) To bring Daniel the answer to his prayer.
b) That he was 'greatly beloved' (rsv), 'highly esteemed' (niv), 'God loves you very much' (lb), 'He loves you (gnb).

DAY 7 a) An end to sin and the bringing in of everlasting righteousness.
b) To the death of the Lord Jesus. As someone 'cut off' (niv).

GUIDE TO STUDY 10

DAY 1 a) In the third year of Cyrus' reign.
Cyrus king of Persia had given permission for the exiles to return to Jerusalem and rebuild the temple.
b) A true message about a great war.

DAY 2 a) That it was a pre-incarnation appearance of the Lord Jesus Christ. (Commentators vary in their interpretation of this person.)
b) A figure like a man; robe with gold sash; eyes like fire; legs (feet) like bronze; an unusual voice.

DAY 3 a) Daniel's friends did not see the vision, but were overwhelmed with terror and ran and hid. Paul's companions heard the voice but stood speechless.
b) He became weak and faint, and collapsed on the ground. A hand touched him and raised him to his feet.

DAY 4 a) Three weeks.
b) On the very first day.
c) Three weeks.
There may be hindrances of which we are totally unaware, but we can know that God always hears our prayers.

DAY 5 a) The heavenly visitor carrying the news had been opposed by the prince of Persia.
b) He was one of the chief princes who provided much needed help against the prince of Persia.
c) Angels and human beings are involved in the same conflict. Men have the help of angels and access to the whole armour of God. Victory is possible through the death of the Lord Jesus.

DAY 6 a) To explain to Daniel what would happen to God's people in the future.
b) Words were put in their mouths enabling them to speak.
c) The Holy Spirit.

DAY 7 a) With the evil princes (spirits) of Persia and then Greece.
b) The Book of Truth. The fact that God has written down all future events before they happen.

GUIDE TO STUDY 11

No answers for DAYS 1, 2, 3.

DAY 4   a) He was contemptible, despicable, deceitful, gaining power by lies and intrigue.
b) God's appointed time will overrule all the plans of men, and events will unfold according to His will.

DAY 5   a) Those who have violated the covenant (abandoned their religion); and the people who know their God (follow God).
b) Wise people will share their faith, but some will be killed, some robbed, some made prisoners. They will receive a little help, and will be purified and made spotless.

DAY 6   a) Israel is in between these two great nations, and the troops would have had to march through their land.
b) They were His chosen people, and He had promised that one day the Anointed One would come from them and would be a blessing for the whole earth.

DAY 7   a) God knows exactly what is going to happen. (Remember the Book of Truth, Dan. 10:21?). Not only that, but God plans what is going to happen to work out His purposes. Men of power do as they please, that is, have complete free will, yet God has determined beforehand what will happen!
b) 'God worked His purposes out through the interaction of all these kings and their families, respecting their freedom and giving them each room for responsible decisions ... It would not be true to the rest of the Bible, were we to imagine God decreeing these events exactly beforehand, and then making them happen by simply treating the humans involved as if they were marionettes.' Quotes from *The Lord is King*, by Ronald Wallace.

GUIDE TO STUDY 12

DAY I   a) Pride, exalting himself even above God.
b) The antichrist.

DAY 2   a) The time of the end, i.e., the last days. (GNB inaccurate.)
b) The Lord God.

DAY 3   a) They would experience distress, but those whose names were written in God's book would be delivered.
b) Great distress and then the coming of the Son of Man in power and glory.

DAY 4   a) The righteous (those who love the Lord), and the others.
b) Only by knowing that you have received the Lord Jesus Christ and are living by faith in Him.
(**Leaders**, this could be an opportunity to explain salvation and assurance to non-Christians.)

DAY 5   a) Those referred to in 10:5 as well as Daniel and the two men (angels) – one beside him and one on the opposite bank of the river.
b) As 'astonishing things'.
c) It might be called evasive – he was only told to keep his vision secret.

DAY 6   a) We must be living at 'the time of the end'. God is still working His purposes out but we need to be ready and watchful! (Rev. 16:15).
b) No one knows when the end will come, only God.

DAY 7   That even as Christ's body was raised from death so will the bodies of those who belong to Him. Christians have a living hope of the inheritance which God has prepared for them.

THE WORD WORLDWIDE

We first heard of WORD WORLDWIDE over twenty years ago when Marie Dinnen, its founder, shared excitedly about the wonderful way ministry to one needy woman had exploded to touch many lives. It was great to see the Word of God being made central in the lives of thousands of men and women, then to witness the life-changing results of them applying the Word to their circumstances. Over the years the vision for WORD WORLDWIDE has not dimmed in the hearts of those who are involved in this ministry. God is still at work through His Word and in today's self-seeking society, the Word is even more relevant to those who desire true meaning and purpose in life. WORD WORLDWIDE is a ministry of WEC International, an interdenominational missionary society, whose sole purpose is to see Christ known, loved and worshipped by all, particularly those who have yet to hear of His wonderful name. This ministry is a vital part of our work and we warmly recommend the WORD WORLDWIDE 'Geared for Growth' Bible studies to you. We know that as you study His Word you will be enriched in your personal walk with Christ. It is our hope that as you are blessed through these studies, you will find opportunities to help others discover a personal relationship with Jesus. As a mission we would encourage you to work with us to make Christ known to the ends of the earth.

Stewart and Jean Moulds – British Directors, **WEC International**.

A full list of over 50 'Geared for Growth' studies can be obtained from:

John and Ann Edwards
5 Louvaine Terrace, Hetton-le-Hole, Tyne & Wear, DH5 9PP
Tel. 0191 5262803 Email: rhysjohn.edwards@virgin.net

Anne Jenkins
2 Windermere Road, Carnforth, Lancs., LA5 9AR
Tel. 01524 734797 Email: anne@jenkins.abelgratis.com

UK Website: www.gearedforgrowth.co.uk

DANIEL

· · · · · ·

Christian Focus Publications
publishes books for all ages

Our mission statement –

STAYING FAITHFUL
In dependence upon God we seek to help make His infallible word, the Bible, relevant. Our aim is to ensure that the Lord Jesus Christ is presented as the only hope to obtain forgiveness of sin, live a useful life and look forward to heaven with Him.

REACHING OUT
Christ's last command requires us to reach out to our world with His gospel. We seek to help fulfil that by publishing books that point people towards Jesus and help them develop a Christ-like maturity. We aim to equip all levels of readers for life, work, ministry and mission.

Books in our adult range are published in three imprints.

Christian Focus contains popular works including biographies, commentaries, basic doctrine, and Christian living. Our children's books are also published in this imprint.

Mentor focuses on books written at a level suitable for Bible College and seminary students, pastors, and other serious readers; the imprint includes commentaries, doctrinal studies, examination of current issues, and church history.

Christian Heritage contains classic writings from the past.

For details of our titles visit us on our website
www.christianfocus.com

Christian Focus Publications Ltd
Geanies House, Fearn, Tain,
Ross-shire, IV20 ITW, Scotland, United Kingdom.
info@christianfocus.com